READY, SET, DRAW!

SPACESHIPS, ALIENS, AND ROBOTS YOU CAN DRAW

Nicole Brecke

Patricia M. Stockland

M Millbrook Press / Minneapolis

The images in this book are used with the permission of: © iStockphoto.com/Dzianis Miraniuk, p. 4; © iStockphoto.com, pp. 4, 5, 23; © iStockphoto.com/Boris Yankov, p. 5; © iStockphoto.com/ JR Trice, p. 5; © iStockphoto.com/Tobias Helbig, p. 7; © iStockphoto.com/Tamara Kulikova, p. 9; © iStockphoto.com/Tina Rencelj, p. 11; © iStockphoto.com/Andreas Gradin, p. 15; © iStockphoto.com/ Shaun Lombard, p. 19; © iStockphoto.com/Perry Kroll, p. 27; © iStockphoto.com/Lars Lentz, p. 31.

Front cover: © iStockphoto.com/Tobias Helbig (desert); © iStockphoto.com/Perry Kroll (Mars); © lofoto/Dreamstime.com (hand).

Edited by Mari Kesselring

The publisher wishes to thank Marcel Bergerman of Carnegie Mellon University for serving as a consultant on this title.

Millbrook Press
A division of Lerner Publishing Group, Inc.
241 First Avenue North
Minneapolis, MN 55401 U.S.A.

Website address: www.lernerbooks.com

Library of Congress Cataloging-in-Publication Data

Brecke, Nicole.
    Spaceships, aliens, and robots you can draw / by Nicole Brecke and Patricia M. Stockland ; illustrated by Nicole Brecke.
        p.   cm. — (Ready, set, draw!)
    Includes index.
    ISBN: 978–0–7613–4167–3 (lib. bdg. : alk. paper)
    1. Outer space in art—Juvenile literature. 2. Science fiction in art—Juvenile literature.
3. Drawing—Technique—Juvenile literature. I. Stockland, Patricia M. II. Title.
NC825.O9B74 2010
741.2—dc22   2009023996

Manufactured in the United States of America
1 – BP – 12/15/2009

TABLE OF CONTENTS

ABOUT THIS BOOK

Cyborgs, robots, and UFOs! Whether real or unknown, these creations are out of this world! With the help of this book, you can start sketching your own science-driven designs. Soon you'll know how to create many different spaceships and robots.

Follow these steps to create each robot, alien, or spaceship. Each drawing begins with a basic form. The form is made up of a line and a couple of shapes. These lines and shapes will help you make your drawing the correct size.

A First, read all the steps and look at the pictures. Then use a pencil to lightly draw the line and shapes shown in RED. You will erase these lines later.

B Next, draw the lines shown in BLUE.

C Keep going! Once you have completed a step, the color of the line changes to BLACK. Follow the BLUE line until you're done.

WHAT YOU WILL NEED

PENCIL SHARPENER

COLORED PENCILS

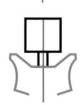

HELPFUL HINTS

Be creative. Use your imagination. Read about astronauts, space shuttles, and robotic dogs. Then follow the steps to sketch your own book of real and unreal science marvels.

Practice drawing different lines and shapes. All your drawings will start with these.

Use very light pencil lines when you are drawing.

ERASER

Helpful tips and hints will offer you good ideas on making the most of your sketch.

PENCIL

Colors are exciting. Try to use a variety of shades. This will add value, or depth, to your finished drawings.

PAPER

Keep practicing, and have fun!

HOW TO DRAW A UFO

What's that in the sky? Could it be an unidentified flying object? If it's a UFO, you could let the National Aviation Reporting Center on Anomalous Phenomena (NARCAP) know. No one knows if UFOs are real. But this group tracks possible UFO sightings as well as other unexplained lights and objects that pilots sometimes see. Movies often show UFOs as round, shiny discs that can hover in the air and then quickly disappear. This is where the term *flying saucer* likely comes from. Make your own imaginary UFO!

1 Lightly draw a wide base oval. Add a baseline. Outline the oval, and add a curved line.

2 Draw a flattened curve. Add a smaller curved line on top to make the cabin.

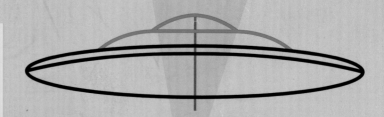

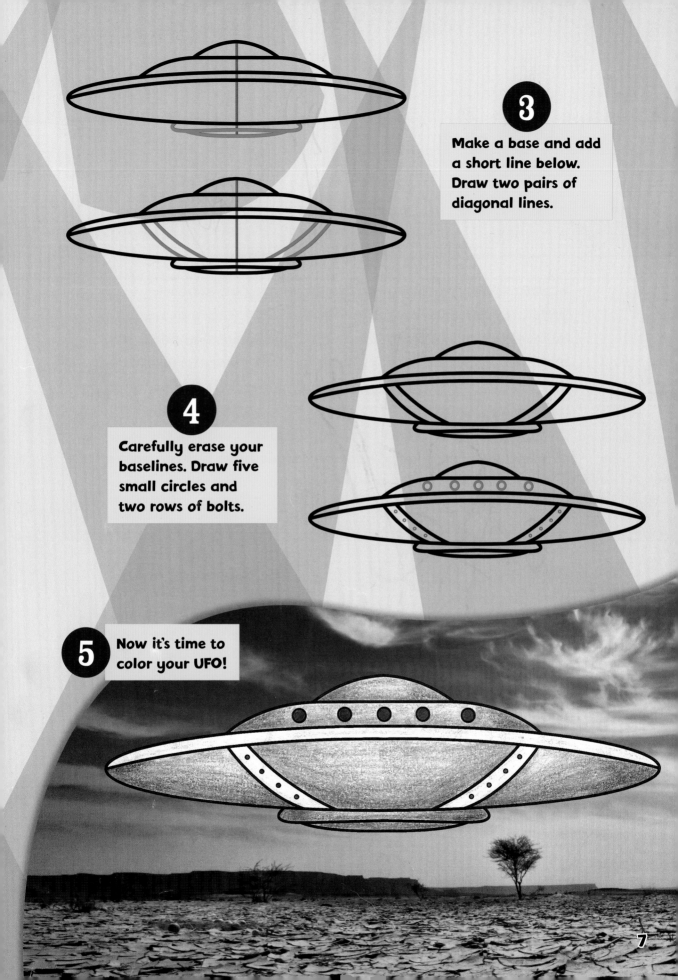

7

HOW TO DRAW AN ALIEN

Science and science fiction disagree about whether aliens have visited Earth. Some people believe that aliens exist. They point to ancient wonders such as the Great Pyramids as evidence of these extraterrestrial (not from this world) creatures. Crop circles, or large patterns left in fields, were once thought to be made by alien life-forms. During the last half of the twentieth century, the idea of aliens sparked a lot of interest. People have written books, made movies, and started research groups devoted to aliens. Is your alien fact or fiction?

1 Draw a base circle and a baseline. Make a lumpy circle inside the base circle.

2 Draw a short neck and shoulder. Add an arm and hand using curved vertical lines. Make the side of the body. Repeat this for the other side.

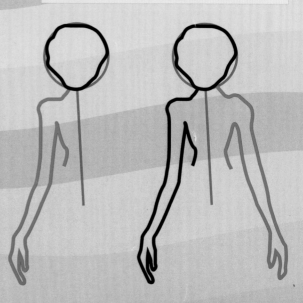

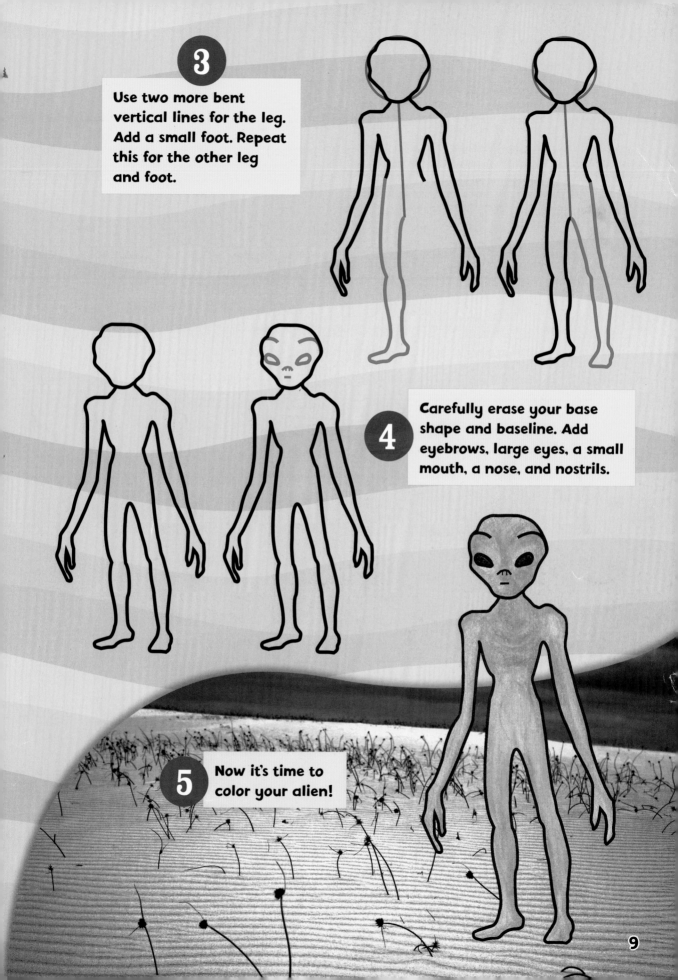

3

Use two more bent vertical lines for the leg. Add a small foot. Repeat this for the other leg and foot.

4

Carefully erase your base shape and baseline. Add eyebrows, large eyes, a small mouth, a nose, and nostrils.

5 Now it's time to color your alien!

HOW TO DRAW A ROBOTIC DOG

Want a friendly pet without the fur? A robotic dog might be for you. This tail-wagging canine is built to obey. A dog robot can be programmed with all kinds of cool features. Teach your techie pet to sit, stay, play dead, or even play soccer! Robotic pets have all kinds of perks, including no need for food. Engineers have created lots of different robotic dogs, each kind with its own set of tricks and tools. Find the perfect robotic pooch for you.

1 Draw a base oval and a curving baseline. Make a wide head shape, narrow muzzle, and ear.

2 Draw a body with a flat belly. Add a tail. Draw the faceplate, and add a nose line.

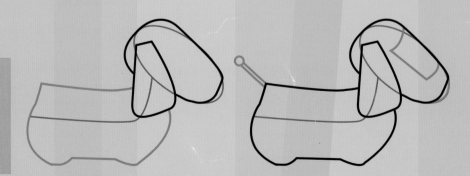

3

Make two matching, bumpy legs and paws. Add the other two legs using bent lines.

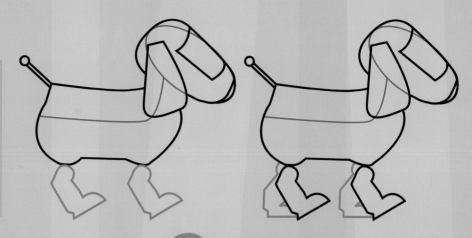

4

Carefully erase your baseline and shape. Draw two circles and three short lines on the forward legs for bolts and joints.

5 Now it's time to color your robotic dog!

HOW TO DRAW A GIANT ROBOT

Large, ultramodern, and sleek, a giant robot is an eye-catching feat of technology. Movies aren't the only place to see giant robots at work. Many industries use robots instead of humans to do dangerous or dirty jobs. Robots are also handy helpers in research and safety testing. Thanks to the help of computers, scientists are able to program robots to do many different tasks. Although this giant robot doesn't exist in real life, you can put your imagination to work creating it now! What can your giant robot help you do?

1 Draw a base square and baseline. Outline the square, and add two short necklines.

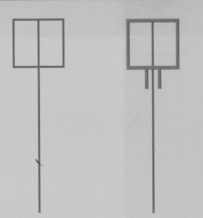

2 Make a curved wing shape for the chest and shoulder on each side. Add a bent line and a horizontal line to each side.

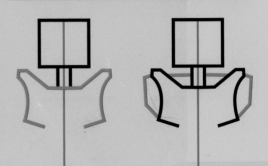

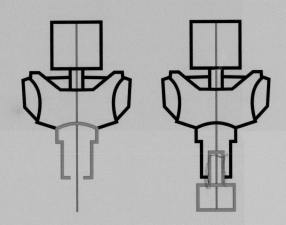

3 Draw an open mushroom shape in the center. Add two rectangles below this.

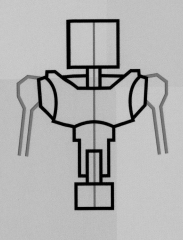

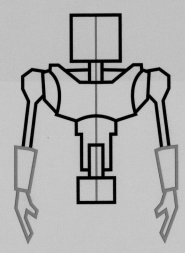

4 Make each arm and shoulder using an oar shape. Add forearms, wrists, and curved hands.

5 Draw an angled rectangle and a knee for each leg. Add a large calf and foot to each knee.

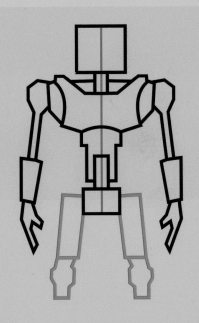

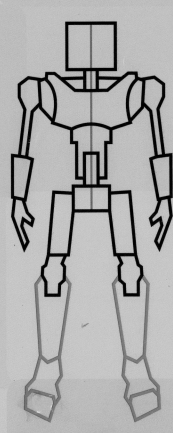

6

Before finishing the face, carefully erase your base shape and baseline. Add a thin, wide rectangle for the eyes and a smaller mouth.

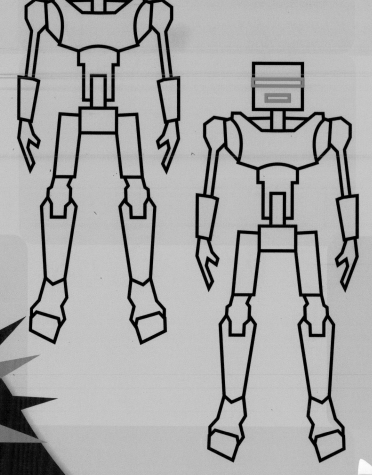

COMMAND CENTER

Even a giant robot needs someone to command the controls.

DRAW A REMOTE CONTROL!

A

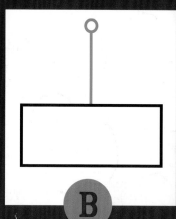

B

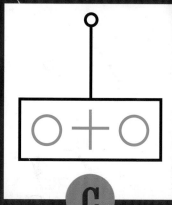

C

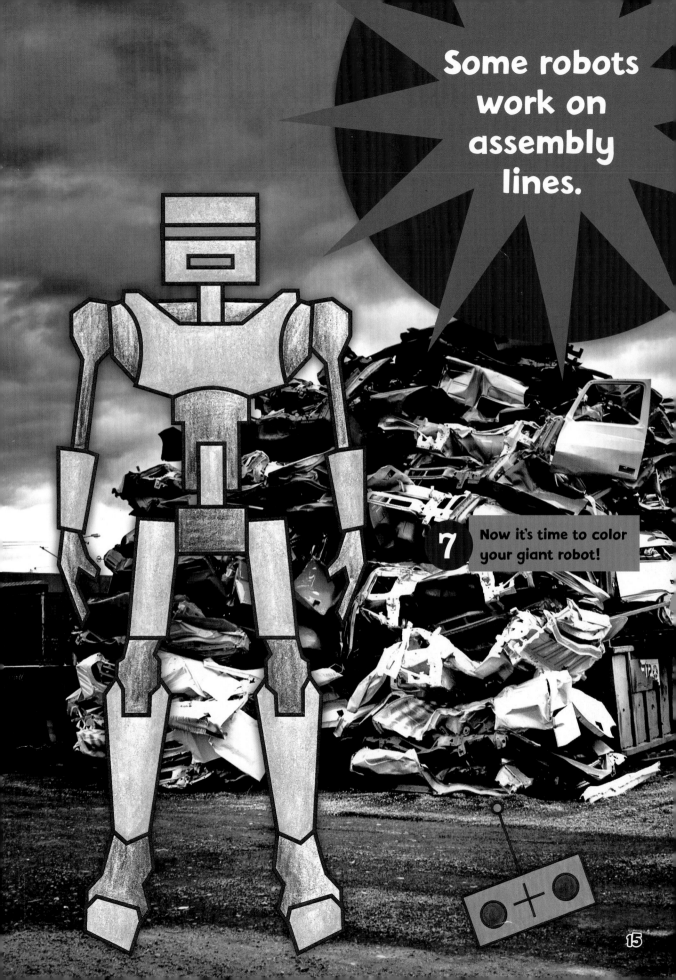

Some robots work on assembly lines.

7 Now it's time to color your giant robot!

HOW TO DRAW A CYBORG

Cyborgs are part human, part robot, and totally amazing. These machines stretch the limits of what might be possible when nature mixes with technology. Movies have shown cyborgs as creatures from the future. But the modern medical field actually uses robotic parts to help people with injuries. No one knows what the future holds for these medical marvels. But you can create your own cyborg now.

1 Draw a base oval and a baseline. Add a half-circle shape to the top.

2 Draw a smaller half circle and two curved lines. Make a bumpy M shape.

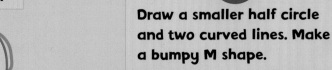

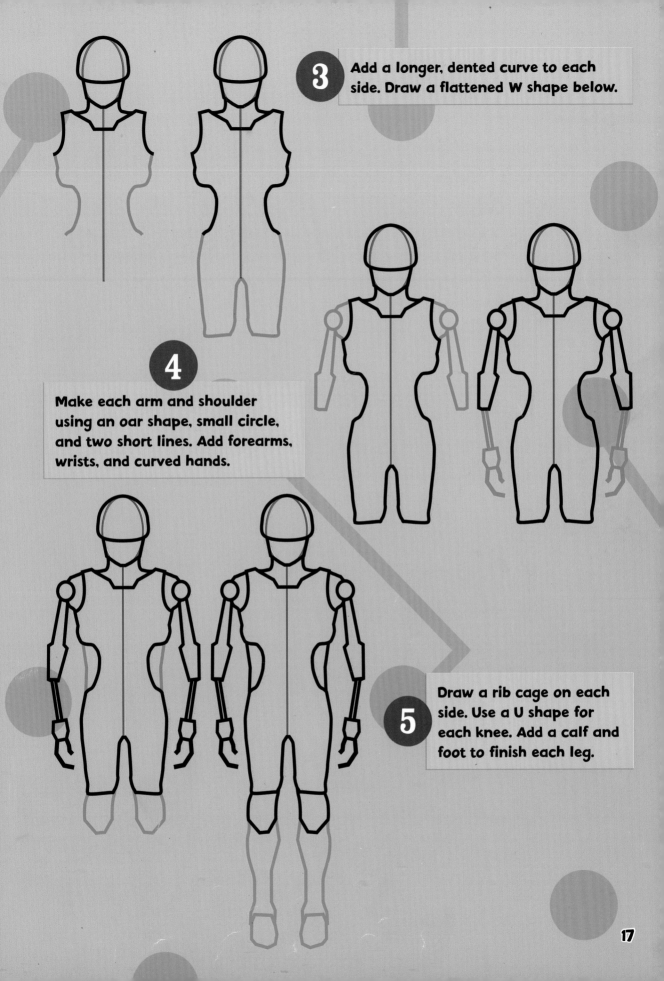

3 Add a longer, dented curve to each side. Draw a flattened W shape below.

4 Make each arm and shoulder using an oar shape, small circle, and two short lines. Add forearms, wrists, and curved hands.

5 Draw a rib cage on each side. Use a U shape for each knee. Add a calf and foot to finish each leg.

6

Carefully erase your base shape and baseline. Draw a curved horizontal line for an eye opening. Add a nose and mouth. Draw two parallel lines on each knee.

Did you know...

THE 1970s TV SHOW *THE SIX MILLION DOLLAR MAN* PORTRAYED A FICTIONAL CYBORG.

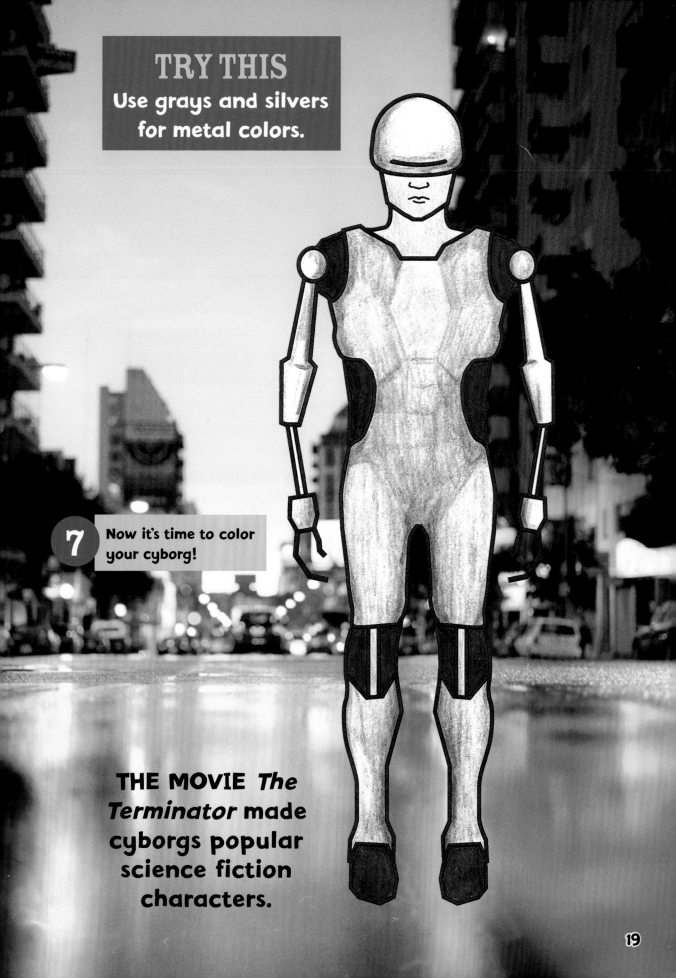

TRY THIS
Use grays and silvers for metal colors.

7 Now it's time to color your cyborg!

THE MOVIE *The Terminator* made cyborgs popular science fiction characters.

19

HOW TO DRAW AN ASTRONAUT

If you want to explore space, then you should think about becoming an astronaut. The National Aeronautics and Space Administration (NASA) trains smart, brave people to explore our solar system. Astronauts often have backgrounds as pilots, engineers, and scientists. NASA chose the first seven U.S. astronauts in 1959. Since then, a total of 321 people have become U.S. astronauts. These busy space pioneers have manned shuttle missions, landed on the moon, and done research at the International Space Station. What exciting mission will your astronaut accept?

1

Draw a base circle and an angled baseline. Make a face shield. Add a bumpy line for the helmet and back.

2

Draw a small rectangle below the face shield. Add two horizontal lines and two vertical lines. Make an arm and a hand. Add the other hand and a short line.

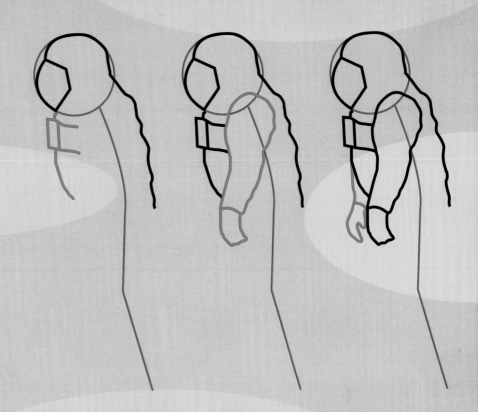

3

Use two long, bumpy vertical lines to make the first leg. Add a big boot. Use two more bumpy lines for the other leg. Add the other boot. Draw a large rectangular pack.

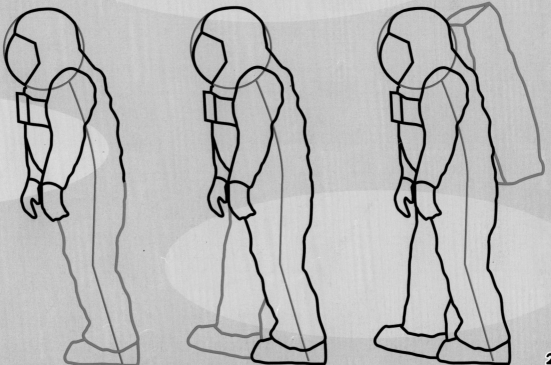

4

Before adding details, carefully erase your baseline and shape. Outline the face shield with a half circle. Add three small lines to the pack.

MOON LANDING

When U.S. *Apollo 11* astronauts landed on the moon in 1969, they planted the U.S. flag there.

DRAW A FLAG!

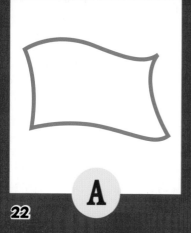

A

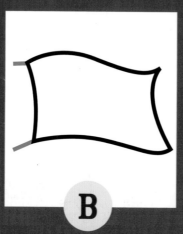

B

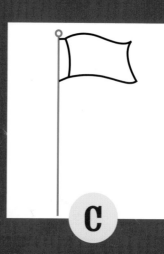

C

TRY THIS
Add small lines to show creases in the space suit.

5 Now it's time to color your astronaut!

THE GREEK WORDS for *space* and *sailor* were combined to create the word *astronaut.*

HOW TO DRAW A
MARS ROVER

Do you ever wonder what's happening on Mars?
Check out images sent from the Mars rovers. These high-tech robots are busy exploring the surface of the red planet. In January 2004, two rovers named *Spirit* and *Opportunity* landed on Mars. The robots work as geologists, exploring the planet's soil, rocks, and landscape. But they're also photographers. Each rover is equipped with a camera, an imager, and other scientific tools. The rovers are able to send images of Mars and other information back to Earth. Make your own Mars rover!

1 Draw a base rectangle and a vertical baseline. Add a hexagon and two parallel lines to the top. Draw a cuff shape and a small U below that.

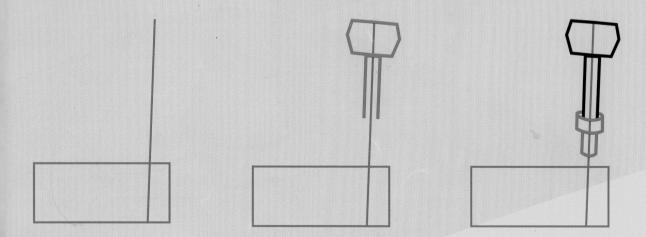

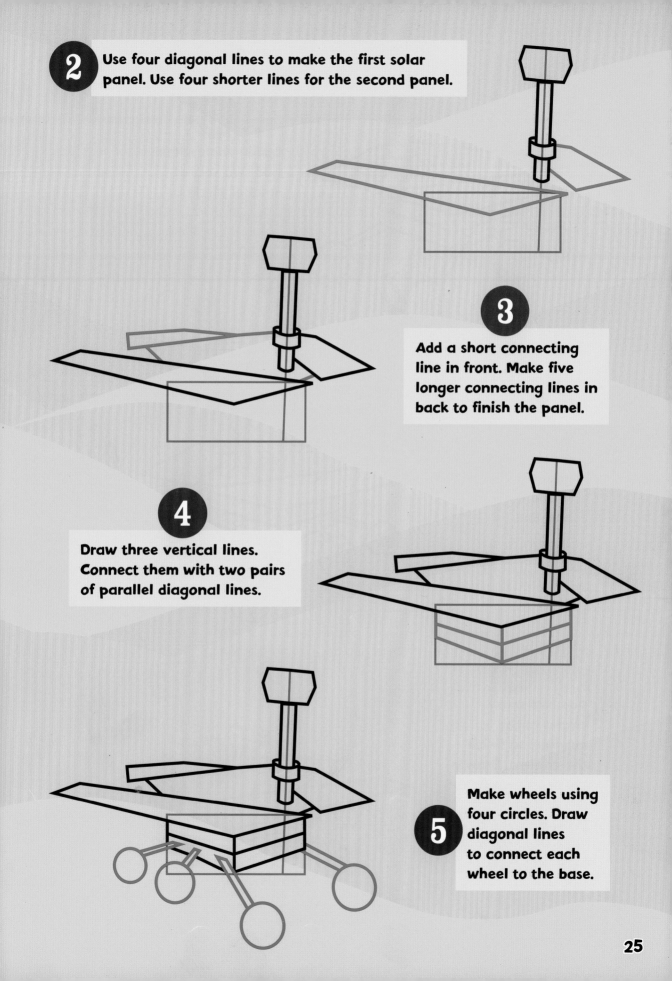

2 Use four diagonal lines to make the first solar panel. Use four shorter lines for the second panel.

3 Add a short connecting line in front. Make five longer connecting lines in back to finish the panel.

4 Draw three vertical lines. Connect them with two pairs of parallel diagonal lines.

5 Make wheels using four circles. Draw diagonal lines to connect each wheel to the base.

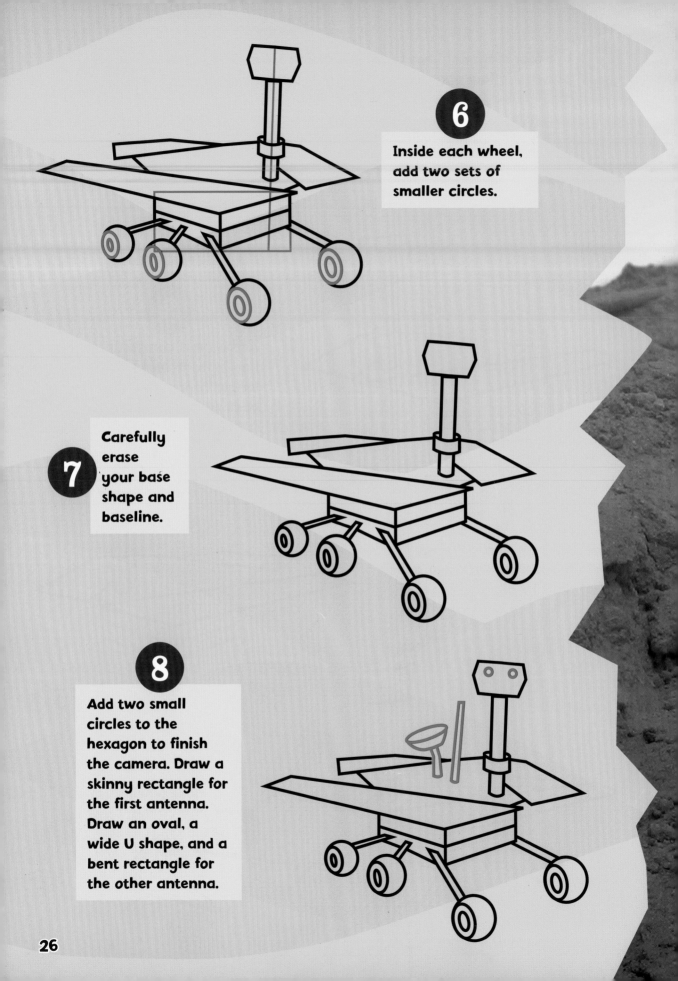

6

Inside each wheel, add two sets of smaller circles.

7 Carefully erase your base shape and baseline.

8

Add two small circles to the hexagon to finish the camera. Draw a skinny rectangle for the first antenna. Draw an oval, a wide U shape, and a bent rectangle for the other antenna.

Special tools allow the rovers to examine soil and rocks close-up.

HELPFUL HINT
Use a variety of colors to create depth.

HOW TO DRAW A
SPACE SHUTTLE

The space shuttle is an amazing creation. This NASA engineering marvel has made travel to space faster and safer. The winged, reusable spaceship allows astronauts to fly multiple missions in a familiar craft. The first space shuttle orbiter was *Columbia*. It made its successful test flight in 1981. The NASA shuttle fleet now has *Atlantis*, *Discovery*, and *Endeavour*. Astronauts rely on the shuttles to reach the International Space Station. Each mission is flown in the spirit of exploration. Take your shuttle into space!

1 Draw a wide base oval. Add a diagonal baseline. Draw a wide C shape with a small bump on the top and a bent end.

2

Use curved V shapes for each wing. Add a diagonal line to the front wing and a tiny V shape to the corner.

3 Draw a short curved line. Make two horizontal lines on the side and a short vertical line. Finish the front wing with four angled lines.

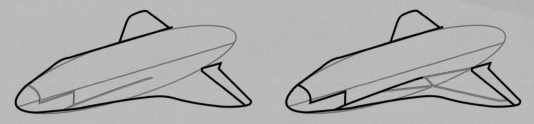

4 Add two curved lines and a longer straight line to the top. Add an M shape and a T shape to the back.

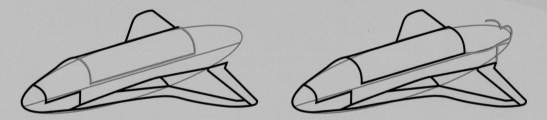

5 Make the tail fin using a small rectangle inside a larger, rounded rectangle. Add a bent line. Draw four curved lines on the back.

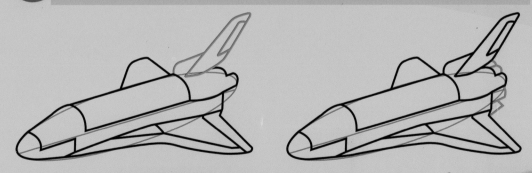

Fast Fact...

IT COST ABOUT
$1.7 BILLION
TO BUILD ENDEAVOUR.

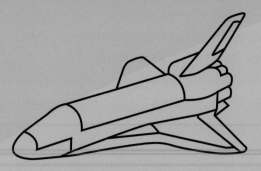

6

Carefully erase your base shape and baseline.

7 Add five windows across the front of the cockpit.

REAL SEAL

Make your space shuttle more authentic by adding the **NASA** logo.

DRAW A LOGO!

A

B

C

TRY THIS

Use gray to add shadows
to your space shuttle.

8 Now it's time to color your space shuttle!

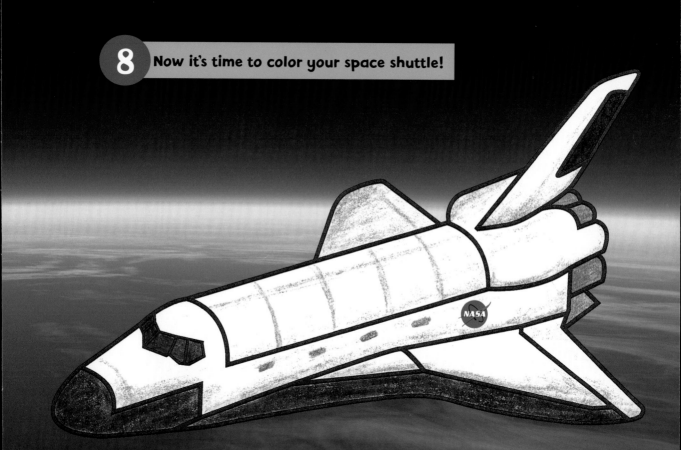

FURTHER READING

Jefferis, David. *Robot Voyagers.* New York: Crabtree Publishing Company, 2006.

Mars Quest Online
http://www.marsquestonline.org/mer/

McPherson, Stephanie Sammartino. *The First Men on the Moon.* Minneapolis: Lerner Publications Company, 2009.

NASA Kids' Club
http://www.nasa.gov/audience/forkids/kidsclub/flash/index.html

NOVA Bomb Squad Robots
http://www.pbs.org/wgbh/nova/robots

Rees, Peter. *Secrets of the Space Shuttle.* Danbury, CT: Children's Press, 2007.

Robotics
http://www.thetech.org/exhibits/online/robotics

Siy, Alexandra. *Cars on Mars: Roving the Red Planet.* Watertown, MA: Charlesbridge Publishing, 2009.

INDEX